PETER ÍLYICH TCHAIKOVSKY

SERENADE

for Strings
für Streicher
Op.48

D1464702

Ernst Eulenburg Ltd
London · Mainz · New York · Paris · Tokyo · Zürich

TSCHAIKOWSKY, SERENADE FOR STRING-ORCHESTRA OP. 48

The Serenade for String Orchestra shows evidence of the influence of German classicism and romanticism upon Tschaikowsky, to a greater extent than the majority of his other compositions. On hearing the first movement, with its heavily-measured Introduction, its first subject *à la* Schumann and its old-fashioned second subject, a listener, unacquainted with the composer, would class him as a German romantic reverting to archaic forms rather than a Russian master. Particularly so with the second movement — a Waltz, which is characteristic of Johann Strauß with additional French grace, and which has many counter-parts in Tschaikowsky's musical out-put. It is not until we reach the Elegy, the longest movement of this generally concise work, that the Slavonic atmosphere becomes apparent, enveloping us completely in the burlesque Finale. Its introduction, together with the first subject entering on the 44th bar are Russian national-possessions. Upon examination it becomes apparent that this first subject of the last movement is closely related to the Introduction to the first movement and is altered harmonically and rhythmically to suit the difference of mood.

There are two peculiarities to be noted with regard to the Serenade. It is striking that a Slavonic composer should write both principal and secondary themes in the major key; it is no wonder that the joyful atmosphere predominates. Leipzig, Nov. 1926.

Further, the sequence of keys is remarkable. It is very rare, in a symphonic work or a work in the form of a suite, to find the separate movements in the key-sequence of C major, G major and D major, in doubled dominant relationship, the one to the other; technical reasons of composition must have governed this procedure. As the Finale had naturally to return to the original key, Tschaikowsky did not revert to the smooth key of C major immediately after the D major close of the Elegy, but took care to work his way through the G major Introduction in order to make a free and natural return to C major.

The Serenade for String Orchestra was composed in the Winter of 1880/81 and dedicated to Konstantin Karlowitsch Albrecht, a friend of the composer in the latter's youth. He was Inspector of the Moscow Conservatoire where Tschaikowsky was appointed teacher of theory by the director Nikolai Rubinstein in the year 1866. Both Tschaikowsky and Rubinstein were boarders in Albrecht's house.

Soon after the first performance of the Serenade at Moscow, the composer wrote from Rome to his brother Anatol as follows: — "On Saturday, Jan. 16th, [1882] Peter Ilitch's Serenade for String Orchestra was given for the first time, conducted by Max Erdmannsdörfer. According to the newspaper articles and letters from Jurgenson [his publisher] it had great success".

Max Unger

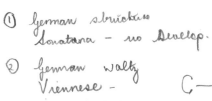

TSCHAIKOWSKY, SERENADE C DUR, OP. 48

Die Serenade für Streichorchester bekundet den Einfluß, den die deutsche Klassik und Romantik auf Tschaikowsky ausübten, in höherem Grade als seine meisten anderen Orchesterwerke. Zumal beim Vortrag des ersten Satzes mit der gewichtigen Schrittes auftretenden Einleitung, dem Schumannschen Hauch atmenden ersten und dem altväterischen zweiten Thema würde einer, der über den Tondichter im unklaren wäre, vielmehr auf einen archaisierend eingestellten deutschen Romantiker denn auf den russischen Meister schließen wollen. Eher schon läßt der zweite Satz an ihn denken: Dieser Walzer, der über die Art eines Johann Strauß französisches Parfüm gießt, hat in Tschaikowskys Schaffen eine ganze Reihe Gegenstücke. Erst in der Elegie, dem verhältnismäßig längsten Satz des im übrigen sehr knapp gehaltenen Werkes, klingt ein slavischer Unterton an, während das burleske Finale einen völlig russischen Nationalcharakter hat. Seine Einleitung wie auch das nach 43 Takten einsetzende erste Thema sind russisches Nationalgut. Wer das Werk nicht genau studiert hat, wird kaum bemerken, daß dieses erste Thema des letzten Satzes melodisch mit der Einleitung des ersten ganz verwandt ist: Tschaikowsky hat es also harmonisch und rhythmisch für die Stimmung des ersten Satzes umgebogen. Noch sei auf ein paar weitere formale Eigentümlichkeiten der Serenade hingewiesen: Bei einem slavischen Tonsetzer muß es besonders auffallen, daß sämtliche Haupt- und Seitenthemen in Dur stehen. Kein Wunder, daß die freudigen Stimmungen überwiegen. Ferner ist die Tonartenfolge sehr auffällig: Daß die einzelnen Sätze eines symphonischen oder suitenartigen Werkes in dieser Serenade mit der Folge C dur, G dur und D dur zweimal im Dominantverhältnis zu einander stehen, ist sehr selten und hat hier sicher seine kompositionstechnischen Gründe gehabt. Natürlich stellte Tschaikowsky das Finale, das wieder in der Anfangsart des Werkes stehen mußte, nicht gleich mit dem glatten C dur des Hauptthemas hinter den D dur-Schluß der Elegie, er trug vielmehr durch die in G dur stehende Einleitung um eine zwanglose Rückkehr nach C dur Sorge.

Die Streichorchesterserenade ist im Winter 1880/81 geschrieben und Tschaikowskys Jugendfreund Konstantin Karlowitsch Albrecht gewidmet. Das war der Inspektor des Moskauer Konservatoriums, wohin Tschaikowsky vom Direktor Nikolai Rubinstein im Jahre 1866 als Theorielehrer berufen worden war. Dieser hatte mit Rubinstein in dessen Hause gewohnt und beide waren früh und mittags Pensionäre Albrechts gewesen. Bald nach der Moskauer Erstaufführung des Werkes schrieb der Tondichter selbst aus Rom an seinen Bruder Anatol: „Am Sonnabend, d. 16. Januar [1882], erlebte Peter Iljitschs Serenade für Streichorchester unter Max Erdmannsdörfers Leitung ihre erste Aufführung und hatte, laut den Zeitungsberichten und den Briefen Jurgensons [seines Verlegers] einen sehr großen Erfolg."

Max Unger

*modes
descending form
of melodic minor*

SERENADE

I. Pezzo in forma di Sonatina

P. Tschaikowsky, Op. 48
1840 - 1893

Handwritten annotations: C major? chord, a minor? — e c a

CD 22 — 48

⁶⁄₈ dance time

Modalism – not sure which key – C major?
A minor? chord vi – minor chord

Nº 857   E. E. 4646   Ernst Eulenburg Ltd

chord lii — echoes, silence, divisi, writ

Em

(36)

MAJ — musical space high. — Second Subject

Allegro moderato. (♩ = 84.)

Divisi: passages of double notes, directing players
eg 1st Violins to divide into groups, & play only 1 note
usually STRINGS.

chromatic colouring

4

5

SECOND SUB — IN DOMINANT i.e. G

90

arpeggi chord

change texture busy tension

hemiolas

G MAJOR
2nd SUBJECT - echo of
1st Sub

circle of 5ths

1 2 | 3   1 | 2 3 | 1   2 | 3
    6 beats

pizzicato = building up
of tensions

END OF EXPOSITION

RECAP

E.E.4646

both 1st & 2d subjects in tonic as expected ✗

change of texture

210

diopolae

SECOND SUBJECT

E. E. 3646

Andante non troppo. (tempo del comincio.)

Return to 1st Subject

E. E. 4646

duet on violins - dance - interlude
phrase extension dance.

see Corelli 21
SB I

II. Walzer

E. E. 4646

all virtuosi / soloists (19) development
not just accomp - like Corelli - small bits
develop +

2nd Subject – modulation

chromatic shifts in tune. hard

NEW – middle section

Dma   E. E 4646   b mi.

sequences! like Corelli
compressing building up of
tension

A

lots of dynamic markings & C blocks - T
see B 4 ♭

1st Subject + countermelody

same key - differently scored.
interwoven parts

E.E. 4646

chain chromatic 4ths staggered.

tenor X

CODA

cello

Gm f   chromatic sequence

E. E. 4646

pedal G in tonic - entries staggered, builds up
orchestral texture - phrase extension

then recedes; chromatic falls.   fragments

disappears

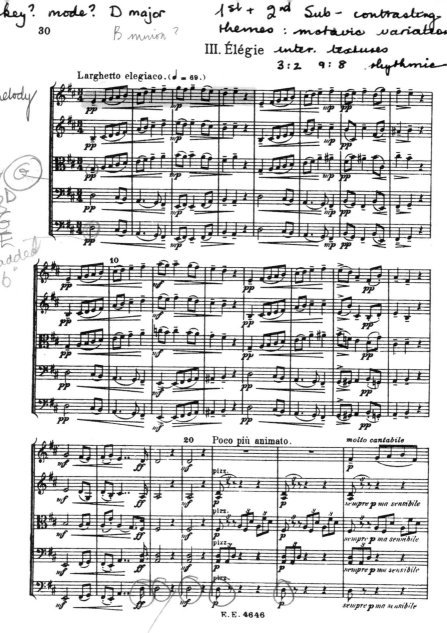

key? mode? D major
30
B minor?

1st + 2nd Sub - contrasting
themes : motavic variations

III. Élégie inter. textures
3:2   9:8   rhythmic

melody

V D C
PAGE
E
added
6°

Larghetto elegiaco. (♩ = 69.)

10

20   Poco più animato.   molto cantabile

pizz.

sempre p ma sensibile

E. E. 4646

now   in D

E. E. 3646

knees up! revisits motivic material - eerie as
muted : simplified

slow introduction

G maj

IV. Finale
(Tema Russo)

staccato &
marcato

Andante. (♩ = 72.)
Con sordini

E. E. 4646

Russian Folksong
transformed balalaiki tune →

E. E. 4646

2nd Subject E♭ MAJOR

Return of 2nd Sub.

E. E. 4646

DEVELOPMENT   combination 1ˢᵗ & 2ⁿᵈ Sub.

46

48

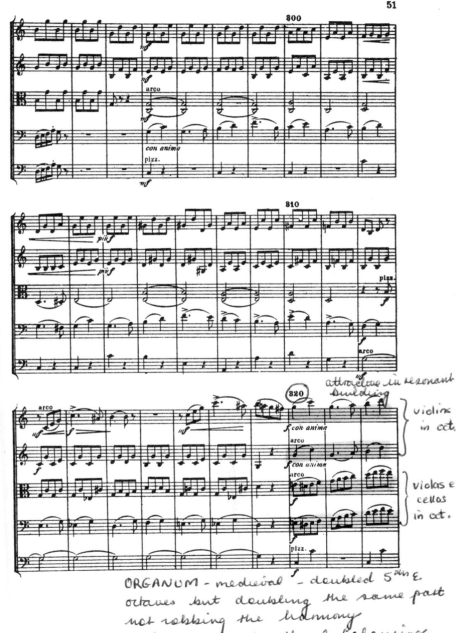

ORGANUM - medieval - doubled 5ᵗʰ & octaves but doubling the same part not robbing the harmony
→ Instrumental & Vocal Colouring.

Molto meno mosso. ♩ ♩ = del comincio.

Mov.t 1

Più mosso.